FROM VIOLIN TO VIOLA

Paul Harris
Jessica O'Leary

ANOTHER STRING
TO YOUR BOW

The essential guide for players moving from violin to viola

FABER *ff* MUSIC

Thanks to the violin students from Eltham College (who now also play the viola!) and to the various Heads of Strings who were so helpful during the conference in Birmingham.

> **Did you know...**
> The phrase 'another string to your bow' is not actually related to string playing but originated from medieval archery practice. Archers carried spare bowstrings, so if one broke, they'd have a backup to continue. By the 1600s, the idiom meant having an additional skill, like playing the viola as well as the violin!

© 2025 by Faber Music Ltd
This edition first published in 2025
Brownlow Yard, 12 Roger Street, London WC1N 2JU
Cover desgin by Chloe Alexander
Text design by Liz Ogden
Music processed by Donald Thomson
Printed in England by Caligraving Ltd
All rights reserved

ISBN10: 0-571-54349-9
EAN13: 978-0-571-54349-6

To buy Faber Music publications or to find out about the full range of titles available
please contact your local music retailer or Faber Music sales enquiries:

Faber Music Ltd, Burnt Mill, Elizabeth Way, Harlow CM20 2HX
Tel: +44 (0) 1279 82 89 82
fabermusic.com

Contents

Introduction

Why playing the viola is a good idea

- The viola's sound quality is very special! It is really beautiful and vibrant, and because the instrument is often larger than a violin it has a deeper (literally lower), richer tone.

- Playing the viola will make you a more flexible and useful musician – you will be able to play first violin, second violin or viola.

- There will be more opportunities to play in chamber music ensembles, which will help you to develop a better understanding of inner parts in ensembles and orchestras.

- You will be able to play violin and cello repertoire on your viola, for example all those wonderful unaccompanied Bach works.

- Being a viola player may also give you a greater chance of securing school or conservatoire scholarships as there are fewer viola players about! And because you play the less common viola, there are more chances to play in advanced groups. Sometimes schools may be willing to buy a viola and loan it out.

The great violinist and teacher, Jascha Heifetz, encouraged all his violin pupils to play the viola too, and playing both instruments is standard practice in several music schools, conservatoires and countries. In addition, many great violin soloists have also played the viola; among them are Nigel Kennedy, Julianne Lee, Zoe Martin-Doike, Yehudi Menuhin, Shlomo Mintz, Niccolò Paganini, Maxim Vengerov, Violeta Vicci, Frank Peter Zimmermann and Pinchas Zuckerman.

Several great composers were viola players, including Bach, Mozart, Beethoven and Dvořák. There are many wonderful performers who are viola soloists, including Yuri Bashmet, William Primrose, Lionel Tertis, Tabea Zimmermann and Nobuko Imai.

Violins and violas – what's the difference?

The main difference between a violin and viola is the size – the viola is generally larger than the violin, is tuned a fifth lower and uses a different clef. Both have 4 strings, but because the viola has thicker strings it needs heavier weight and faster bow speed to produce the sound. Viola bows are longer and heavier than violin bows.

The Symphony Orchestra

Viola players normally sit between the second violins and the cellos in both orchestral and chamber groups. In some countries (Germany for example), the cellos and violas swap position.

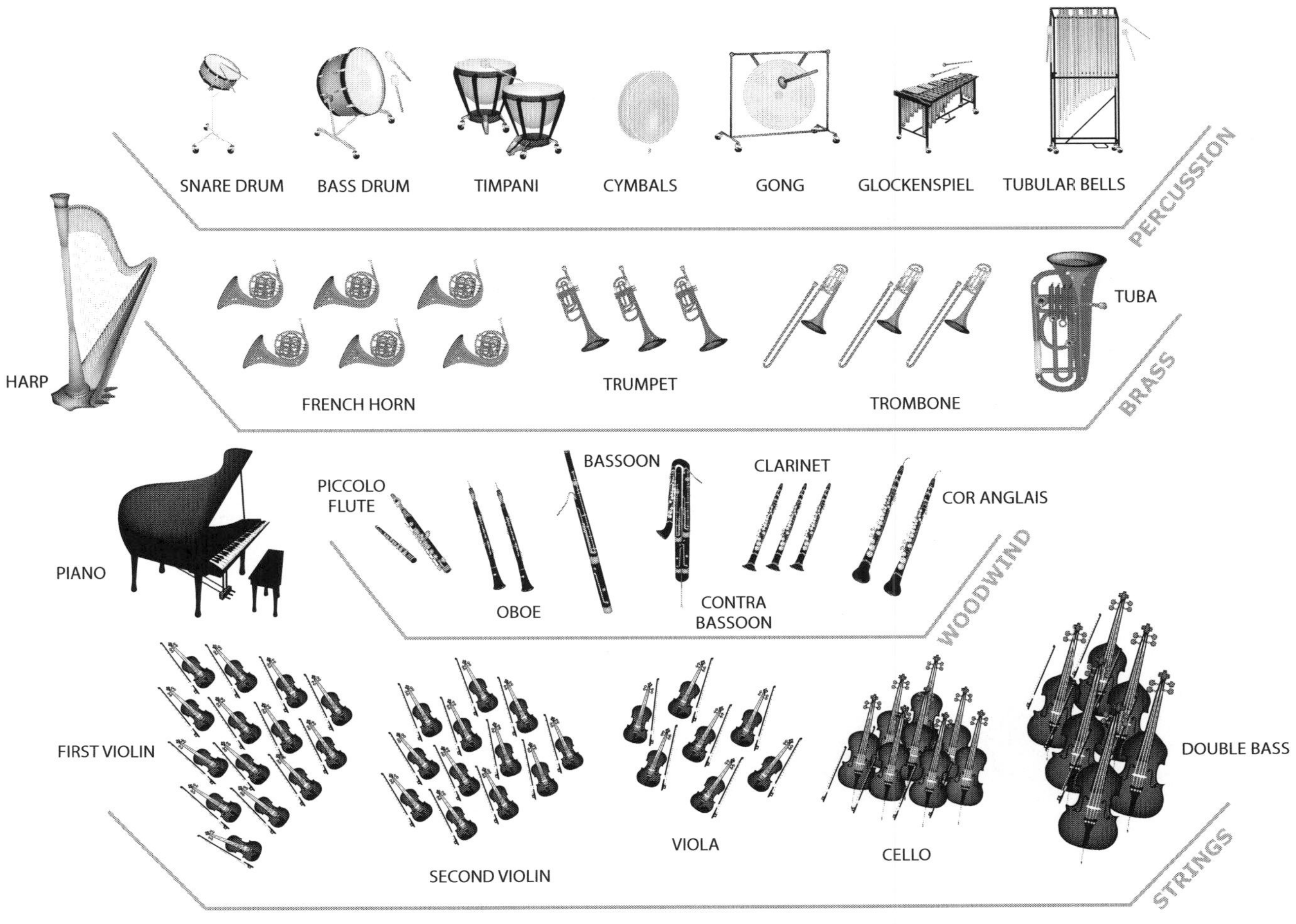

Pre-requisite skills

To enjoy this book, the only pre-requisite skill is simply the ability to play the violin in 1st position and, of course, to have access to a viola!

The ability to shift to 3rd position and possibly use vibrato would be more helpful for the later, more advanced stages of the book.

How to choose the right size of viola for you

You have several options in choosing your viola:

a) Playing a specially manufactured viola which is the same size as your violin, where the bridge and sound post are connected creating a truer viola quality. These are usually termed 'viola conversions'. You can use your violin bow and shoulder rest. This option avoids stretching fingers and often makes for a simple transition.

b) Re-stringing a violin – it is possible to move the A, D and G violin strings and add a short viola C string. This will produce the right pitch but the quality will be slightly compromised. As with option a), you can use your violin bow and shoulder rest.

c) Using a viola which is larger than your violin. Fingers will necessarily be stretched more, you'll need a larger shoulder rest or pad, and the sound will be fuller and project more easily. You'll need a viola bow which is heavier and longer than a violin bow.

If you are frequently swapping between violin and viola, it may be useful for the instruments to be the same size. The most important factor is that the instrument is comfortable.

Violins and violas are traditionally measured in inches:

A three-quarter size violin = 13 inches (33cm)
A full-size violin = 14 inches (35.5cm)
A small viola = 15 inches (38cm)
An average viola = 16 inches (40.5cm)
A large viola = 17 inches (43cm)

Extra useful information

How to upgrade your viola

If you play your viola more often than your violin you may like to have a bigger viola. Your teacher or specialist dealer can help with this. It's essential to play the instrument before you buy it, so avoid buying online.

Because the viola is heavier than a violin you may want to look at different shoulder rest options to give the appropriate control. If you feel your viola slips forward, especially in higher positions, consider a shoulder rest that extends behind the left shoulder to give more support.

How to find a viola teacher

Many violin teachers also teach the viola, but if not, ask teachers or friends for recommendations. Look online but always arrange a consultation lesson before you commit.

Getting started

There are differences in right- and left-hand technique when playing the viola.

Bow hold

First let's consider the bow hold. It's important to make a resonant viola-like tone which is different from your violin sound. To achieve this, we need to use heavier right-arm bow weight.

The *Franco-Belgian* bow hold is often preferred to give good control and allows you to use the more natural weight of the arm. This is particularly helpful when playing with the top half of the bow to keep the tone singing.

The *Franco-Belgian* bow hold

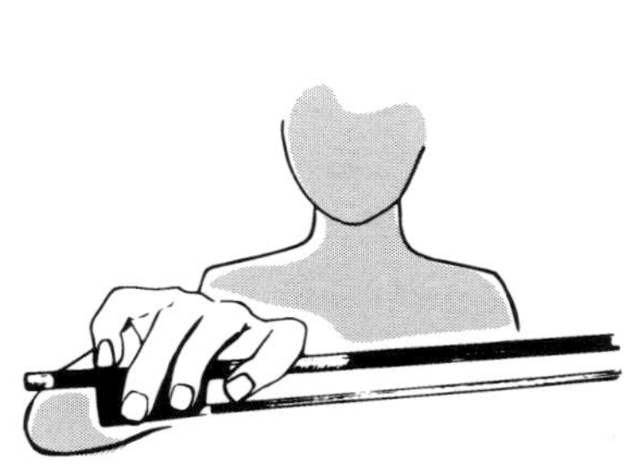
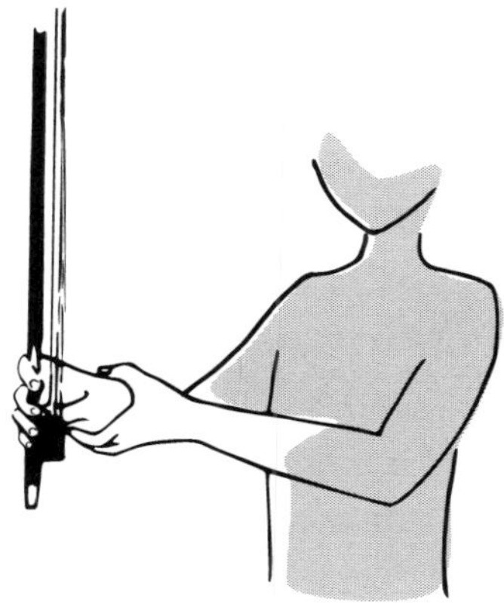

Instrument position

If you are using a viola that is larger than your violin, the instrument position will need to be more flexible in relation to your collarbone so the shoulder is not overstretched. You may like to consider a central chin rest, especially if you have small arms or hands. Experiment with positioning the viola more to the left to rotate your arms more easily when playing on the lower strings.

If you have a small left hand, try swivelling it between notes or even using small shifts between your 1st and 4th fingers. Keep your left fingers light, only pressing as much as needed, and feel the connection and friction between the bow and string. Make sure to take lots of rests.

Viola music is usually written in the alto clef (also called the C or viola clef), although high notes can be in the treble clef.

The history of the alto clef

The alto clef (or C clef) began life in church music of the twelfth century. The letter 'C' was placed at the beginning of the line to literally indicate the pitch 'C'.

Over the years it changed shape, eventually becoming the elegant symbol we see today.

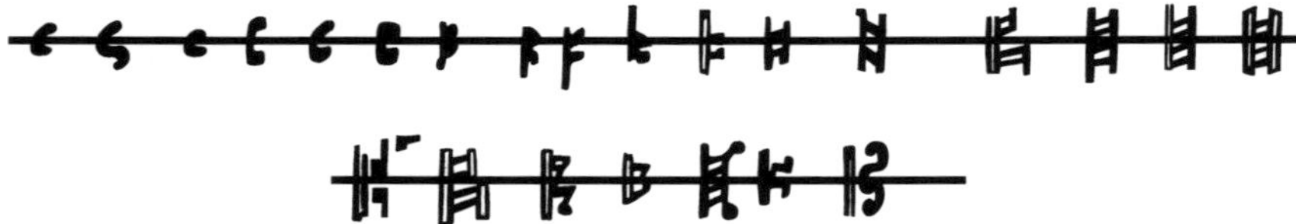

The original 'C' placed around the C line is still visible.

The design of the alto (C) clef shows the note C on the middle line. This is middle C on the piano and we play it with the 3rd finger on the G string when in 1st position.

Here are the note names for reference:

Open strings

Let's begin with the open strings.

The violin strings are **G, D, A** and **E**.

The viola strings are **C, G, D** and **A**.

Memorise the name and position on the stave of these 4 notes:

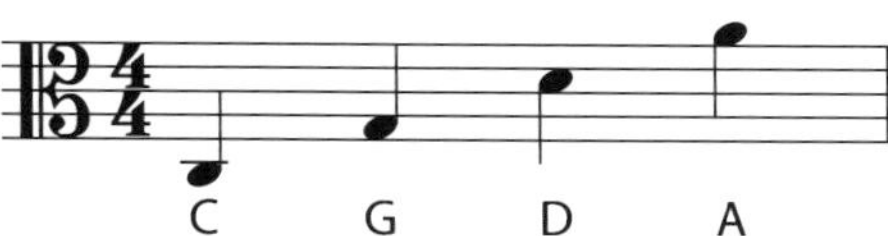

Exercise 1 Enjoy the vibrations when bowing the open strings.

Feel the difference in the weight of your bow arm as you play each string – the lower notes will need firmer contact to keep the string vibrating.

Can you see the C string moving from side to side when you play? Keep the bow carefully positioned between the bridge and the fingerboard and aim to keep it parallel with the bridge. It can be fun to check the bowing action in front of a mirror.

> **TOP TIP**
>
> *In the rests, check that your neck is relaxed.*

Exercise 2 The space between the strings will be wider on a larger viola than on a violin. Play this exercise and feel the difference:

> **TOP TIP**
>
> *Take lots of rests when practising by putting the viola by your side if standing, or on your knees if sitting. It's important to build the muscles slowly so you don't get too tired or lower the scroll too much when playing.*

Stage 2

Reading the viola clef

C major

Play the **scale and arpeggio of C major**, which will feel like playing G major on the violin.

If your viola is larger than your violin, you will feel the space between your fingers is a little wider. Listen to the sound quality and try to look at the strings vibrating. You'll need to add extra weight to your bow arm to create the best quality sound.

Play this scale and arpeggio a number of times, really feeling the position of your fingers *of both hands* so that you are, in effect, re-programming your brain!

TOP TIP

Make strong connections in your mind between the note names and the open strings as you play.

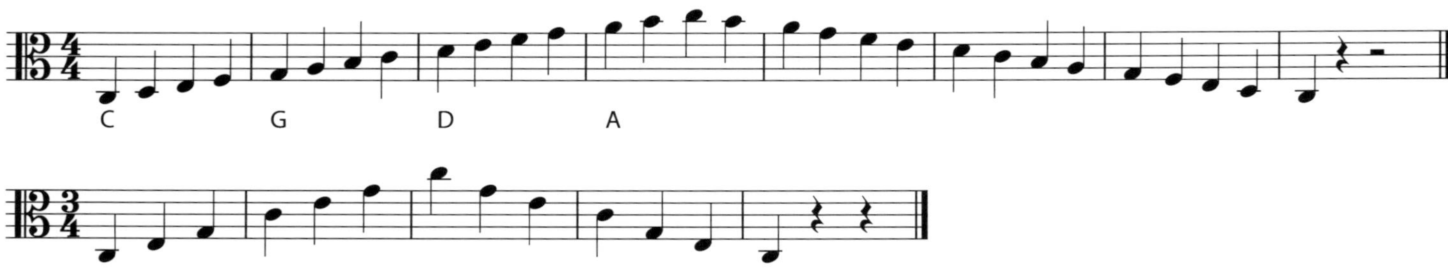

Exercise 3 To develop a resonant viola sound, repeat this C scale exercise varying the bow speed and its position in relation to the bridge.

Use the 4th finger when descending and remember to breathe deeply and steadily; for example, breathe in for one bar and out for the next bar.

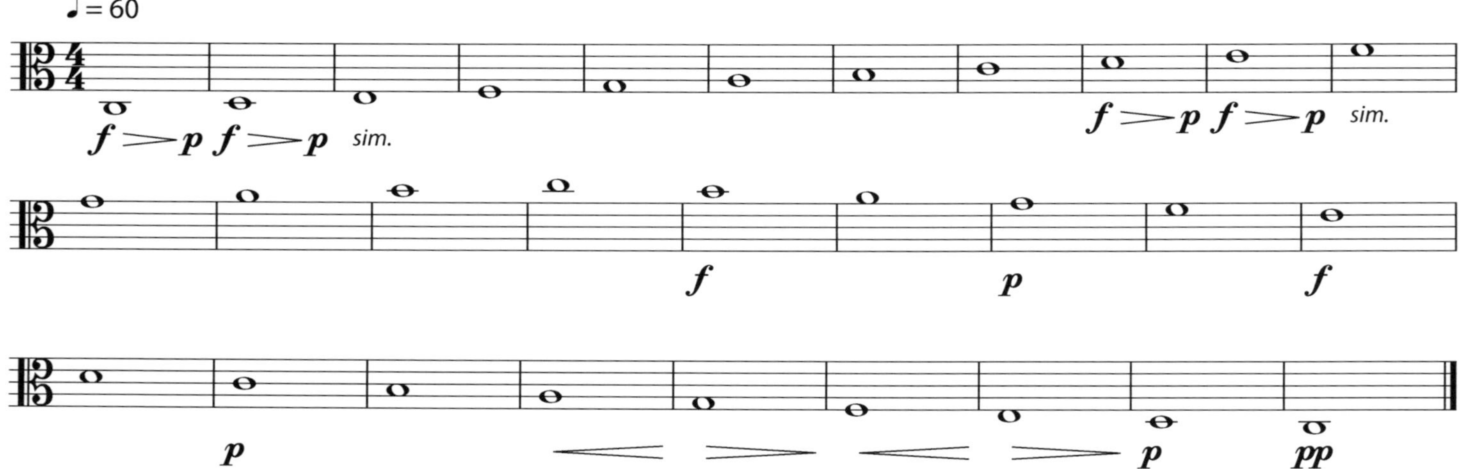

Now play these pieces, also in C major, being particularly aware of the intervals (distance) between notes. Using 4th fingers can help avoid extra string crossing, for example in bar 1.

Don't forget you're playing the viola when crossing to the next line!

Good King Wenceslas

Traditional

Viola boogie

Paul Harris

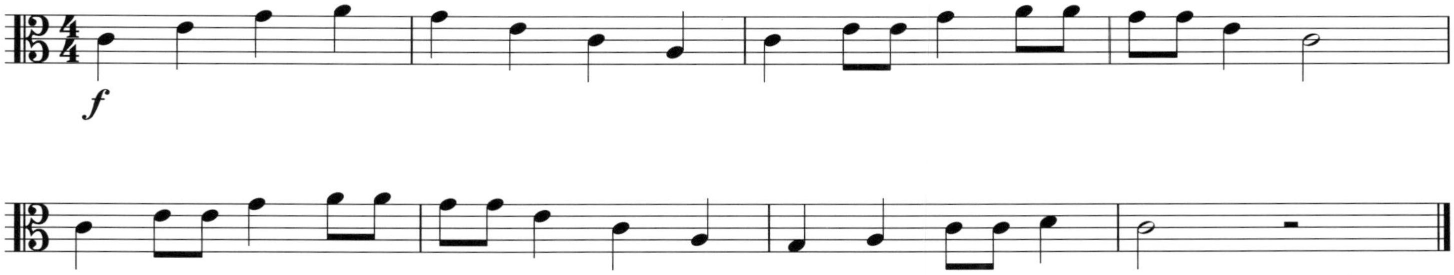

The following exercises increase flexibility which will help with the extra weight of a heavier viola.

1. Forearm flexor lengthening exercise

Gently stretch your right arm out in front of you with your right palm facing upwards. With your left hand apply a light pressure to the fingers in a downward direction. Repeat with the other arm.

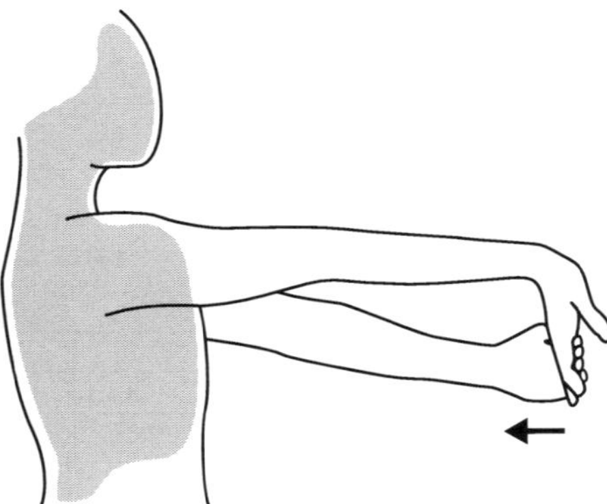

2. Forearm extensor lengthening exercise

Gently stretch your right arm out in front of you with your right palm facing downwards. With your left hand apply a light pressure to the knuckles in a downward direction. Repeat with the other arm.

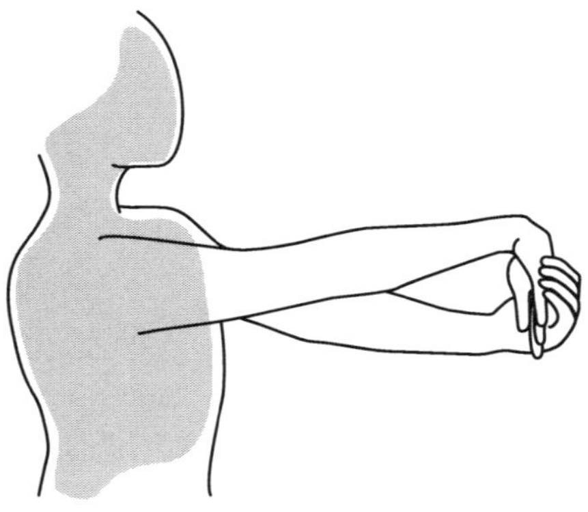

Stage 3

Reading in D major

Here's the **scale and arpeggio of D major**. Play this, again thinking the note names and making your best sound:

Remember that in first position:

- notes on the lines = 1st or 3rd fingers
- notes in spaces = open strings, 2nd or 4th fingers.

Still with your best sound, and thinking the note names, play this piece with character!

Jingle bells

James Pierpont

This piece uses arpeggios – focus especially on the intervals.

Use your best *tremolo* in the top half of the bow in the penultimate bar for a dramatic ending!

Morning has broken

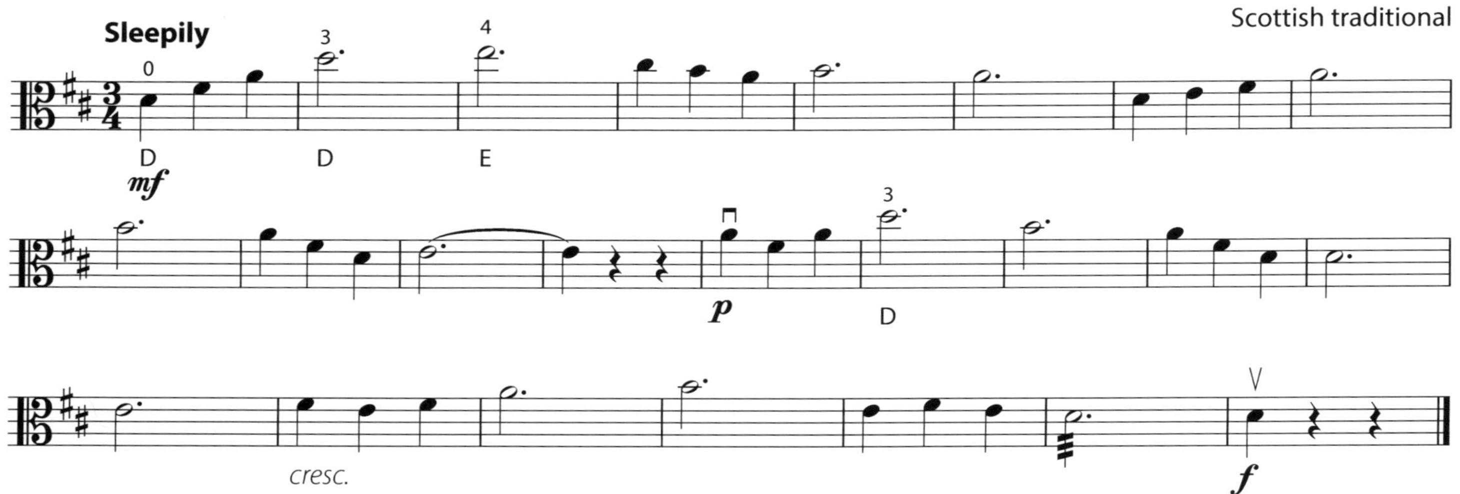

This piece uses high 3rd fingers on the C and G strings for the F♯ and C♯ notes, so remember to rotate both arms and use more bow weight on the low notes to enhance their quality.

TOP TIP

To avoid confusion when changing from the end of one line to the start of the next or onto a new page, consider adding a fingering or note name to keep on track.

Báidín Fheilimí

The title refers to the story of a small boat owned by Fheiliní on its way to Tory Island near Donegal in Ireland.

Stage 4

Rotating arms and placement of the left-hand 4th finger

Here is an extended **scale and arpeggio of G major**. Rotate your arms for the notes on the
C string and notice that your right elbow will be lower on the D and A strings compared
with your violin playing:

Play the following piece thinking the note names and matching the tone on the G string
with the higher octave. Relax your neck in the rests.

Au clair de la lune

This piece is in C major and uses 1st and 3rd positions.

Tambourin

François-Joseph Gossec

Play this movement from Telemann's Viola Concerto slowly at first and try to make your
string crossings as economical as possible.

Notice how the scalic intervals and open strings help in accurate reading. It starts with a
G major arpeggio, followed by shorter scale patterns.

Concerto in G, 2nd movement

Georg Philipp Telemann

16

Intervals

To read music effectively you need to know both the name of the notes and where they can be found on your instrument. Ultimately this should become instinctive. On string instruments there may be one or more fingering possibilities depending on context. Aim to perfect this name/fingering connection.

A good reader is also aware of the intervals between notes. Go back over some of the simpler pieces in this book and play them slowly, thinking about the intervals between each note as you play. Particularly notice scale or arpeggio patterns.

Exercise 4 – Interval instincts Here's a fun exercise to help with reading intervals. As well as knowing the note names and their fingerings, be aware of the interval that you're playing and how that also determines the fingerings. This study uses 3rds and 5ths.

Here's an extended **scale and arpeggio of F major** to play: Relax your left wrist and thumb for the extended 4th fingers. If you have a small hand, allow a slight rocking movement up and down like mini-shifts, rather than stretching and possibly straining the fingers.

Write the note name on top and the interval beneath – the first two have been done for you!

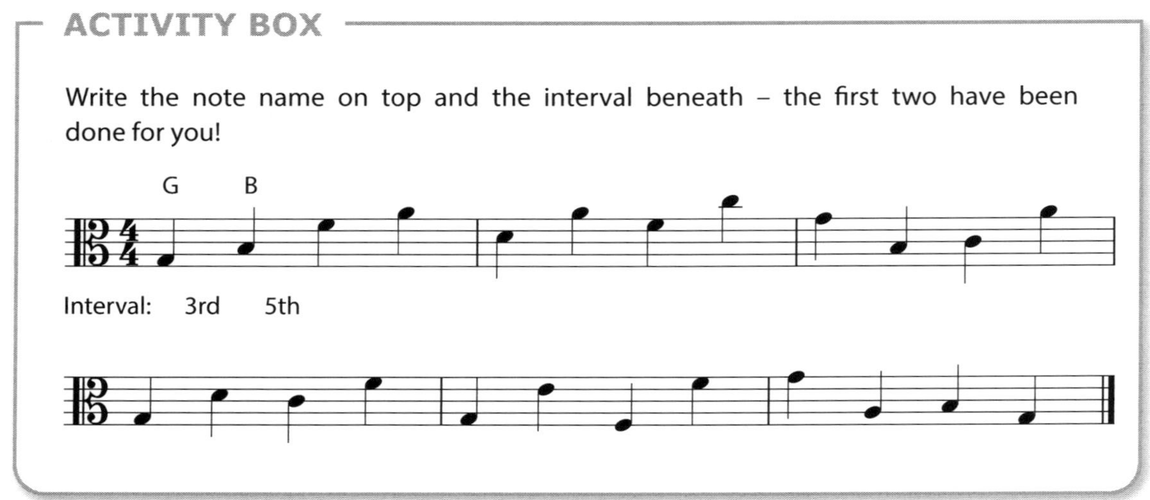

Shifting

Half, 2nd and 4th positions are more common in viola repertoire.

Use smooth shifts when playing this famous tune.

Ode to joy

Exercise 5 Experiment playing this **A minor scale and arpeggio** with *spiccato* bowing.
Notice how the balance point of your bow might feel different when playing it on your violin.

Here's a study with some half-position work:

Sciolto balzato

Allegro spiritoso

Otakar Ševčík

Exercise 6 Play this **scale and arpeggio of D melodic minor** (upside down!).

Here it is again, but backwards!

Bartók wrote many wonderful and useful duets. Use *spiccato* bowing on the quavers.

Slovakian song

Béla Bartók

Stage 6

Control of the top and bottom strings

Exercise 7 These exercises help to develop control of the top and bottom strings.

Start with your bow at the point on the A string and lift it in the air as soon as you've played the short A. Land on C and relax. Think about how your arm moves.

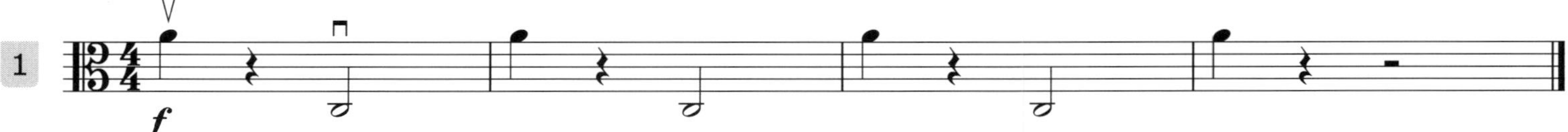

This exercise helps get your arms in the right position for playing on the C string.

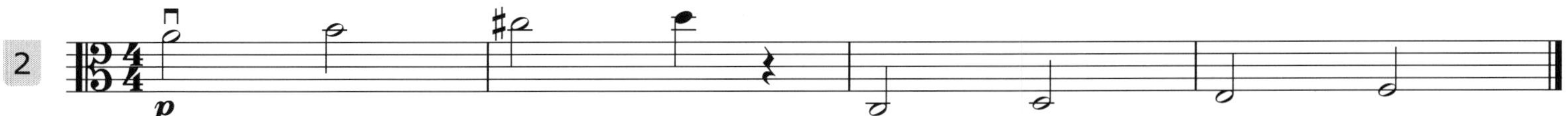

This exercise contains a new C string harmonic. Aim to keep your left elbow at the same angle through the piece.

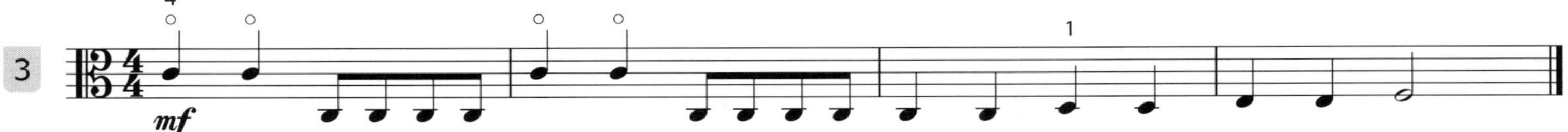

Start this warm-up in the middle of the bow. Play it quite fast and work out how the dynamic changes affect the amount of bow you use.

Enjoy playing the next piece. Notice how the bowing will create the necessary sense of movement to bring the piece to life.

Steam train

Chugging along

Paul Harris

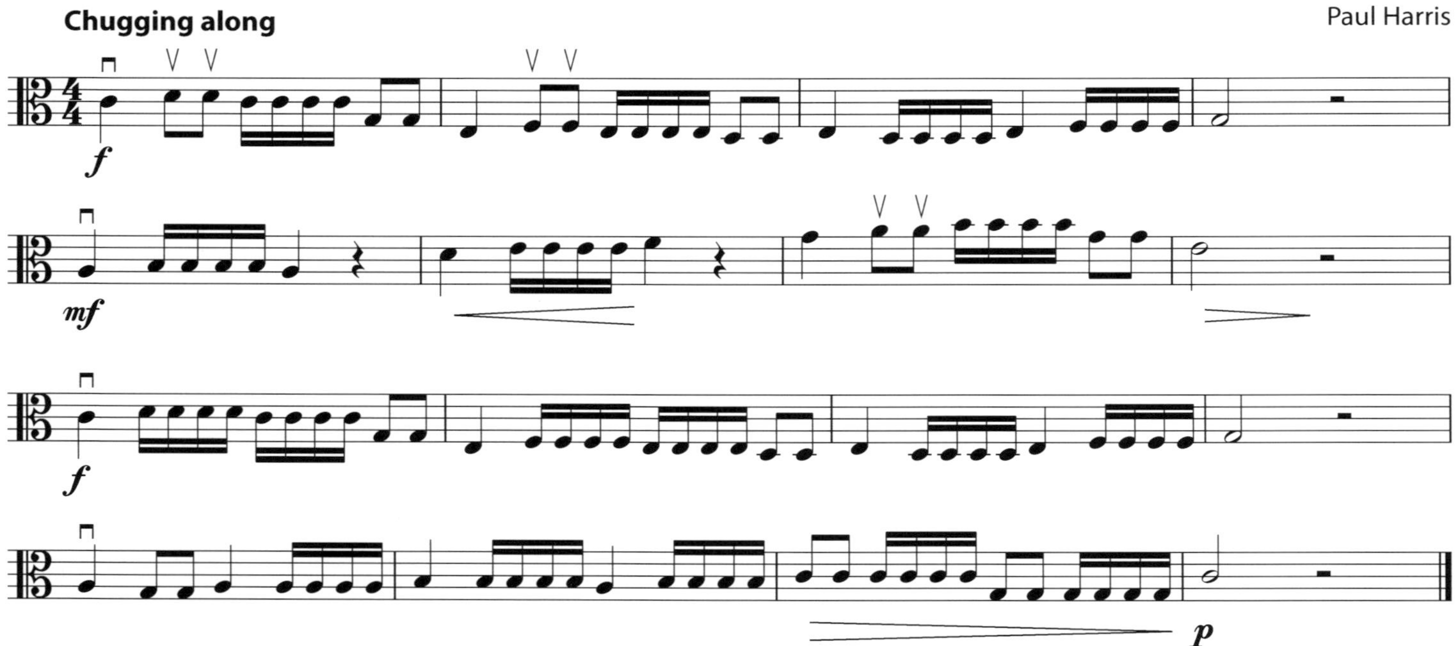

Hold the bow lightly to produce the best character. Be aware of the names of the notes on leger lines and think of them as you play.

The bird catcher's song

Allegro moderato

W.A. Mozart

Stage 7

Vibrato

Viola strings are thicker, making viola vibrato generally slower and wider than violin vibrato.

Here's a good exercise to compare the two.

Exercise 8 On your violin, play an **A major scale** slowly. Use separate bows on the E string, noticing that the speed is faster and amplitude (width) is narrower as the notes go higher to maintain tuning and tonal quality.

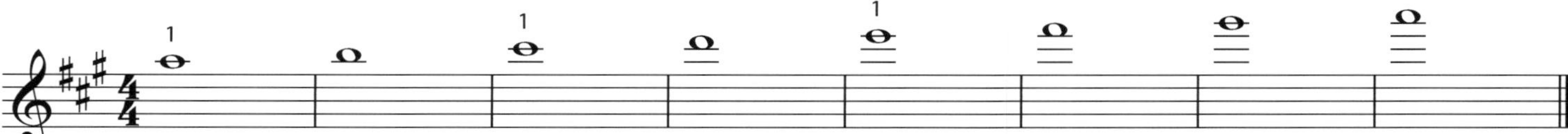

Exercise 9 Now play a **D major scale** on the C string of the viola, similarly with long notes and slow separate bows, one to a note.

Notice that a wider and slower vibrato creates better sound and tonal quality. Imagine vibrato on the double bass which is much slower and wider.

> **TOP TIP**
>
> *Use the fleshier part of your finger pads to help create a wider and slower vibrato.*

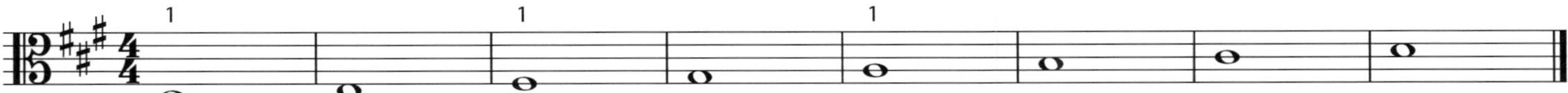

When playing the viola, it takes a little while to develop the motion of wider and slower vibrato.

- For a **wrist vibrato** the movement is similar to rolling dice or waving to yourself.

- For **arm vibrato** it's a little like tapping a nail into a piece of wood with your forearm. Some performers use a combination of wrist and arm vibrato.

- When playing the highest notes **finger vibrato** might be useful at the most advanced levels.

In general, slower and wider vibrato will be most useful when playing on the C string, and the vibrato when playing higher on the A string will be more like that of the violin. As playing the viola becomes more natural you can vary the speed and width to create different tonal colours.

Exercise 10 Experiment with the speed and width of vibrato, and the weight of bow needed, in this very slow scale:

Very slow

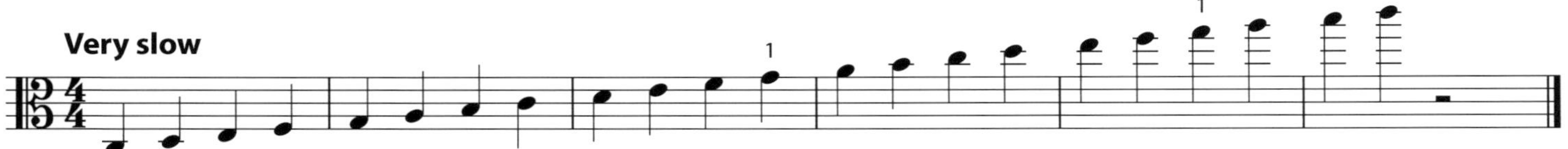

Play this beautiful tune slowly to get the feel of wider vibrato.

Humming song

Largo

Robert Schumann

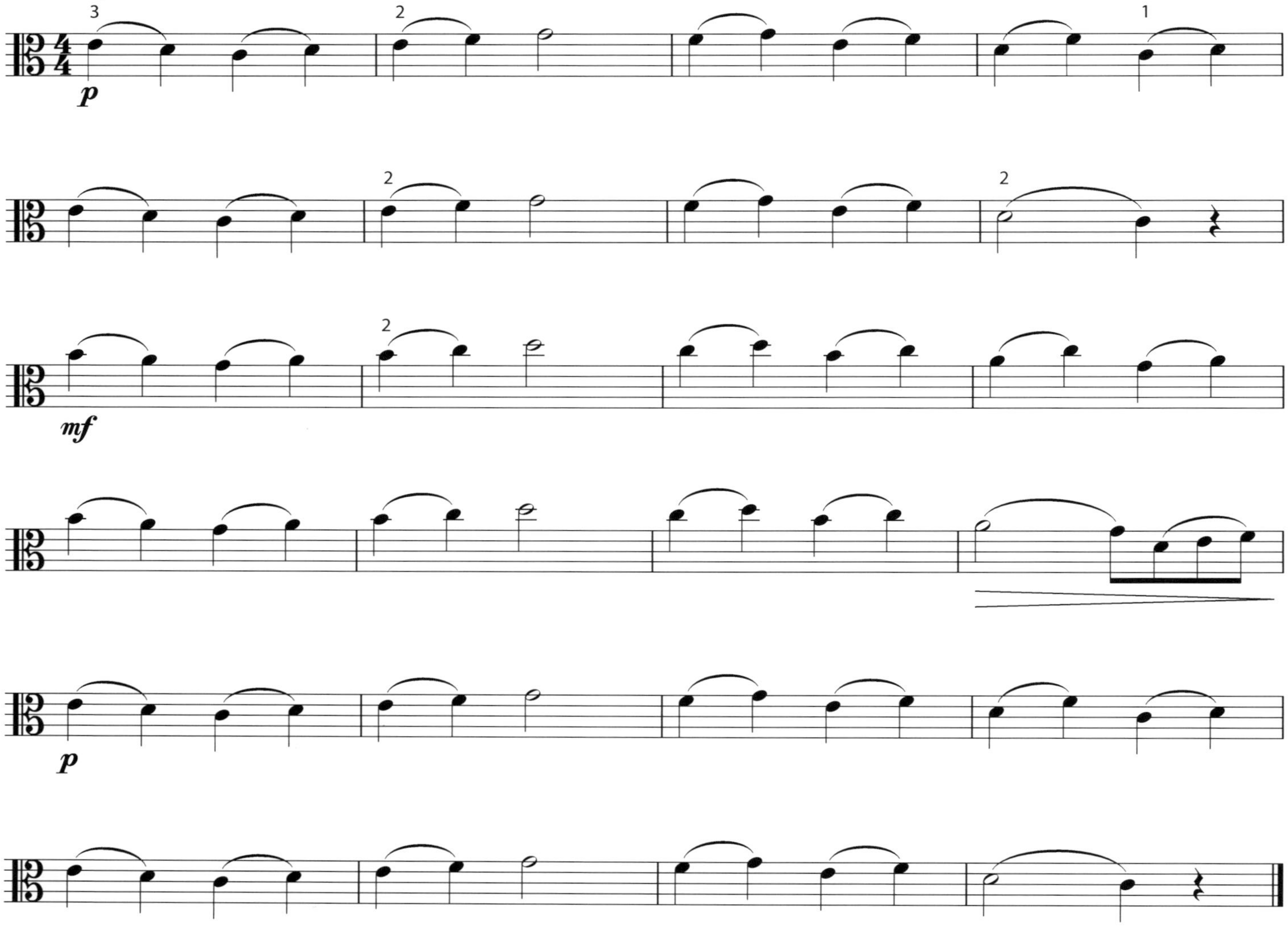

Stage 8

Treble clef, more shifting and high notes

Reading high notes on the viola is often easier in the treble clef than the alto clef. When the music requires a shift up to the high notes it is important to hear the pitch in your head to encourage and facilitate accurate tuning while moving the left hand calmly with a soft thumb.

Exercise 11 Here is a **B♭ major scale** written in the alto clef. Play it slowly with an awareness of the note names and their positions on the stave.

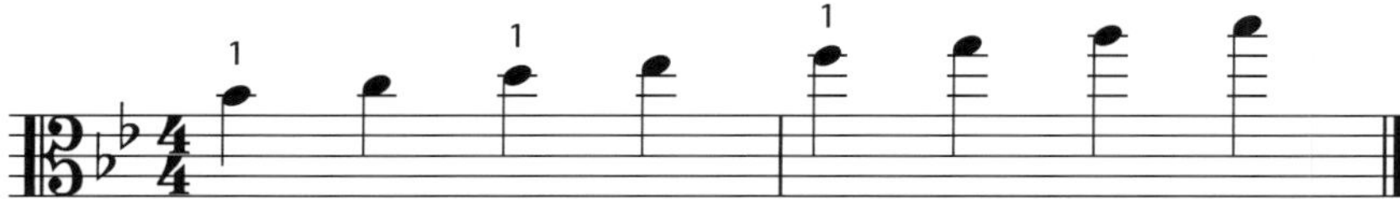

Here it is again in the treble clef. Imagine that you are playing on the A string on your violin. As there is no E string on the viola there will be more shifts.

Exercise 12 Play this exercise slowly with vibrato and with a relaxed left hand. Use plenty of bow during the shift.

> **TOP TIP**
>
> *Remember to keep the left thumb soft to help with the shifts.*

Enjoy playing this famous tune in 1st, 2nd and 3rd positions. If your viola is larger than your violin, the shifts will also be further, so focus carefully on the tuning.

Theme from *The New World Symphony*

Antonín Dvořák

Changing clef

Exercise 13 As a preparation for the next study, play this 3-octave scale and arpeggio of C major. It is common in viola music to change clef mid-phrase.

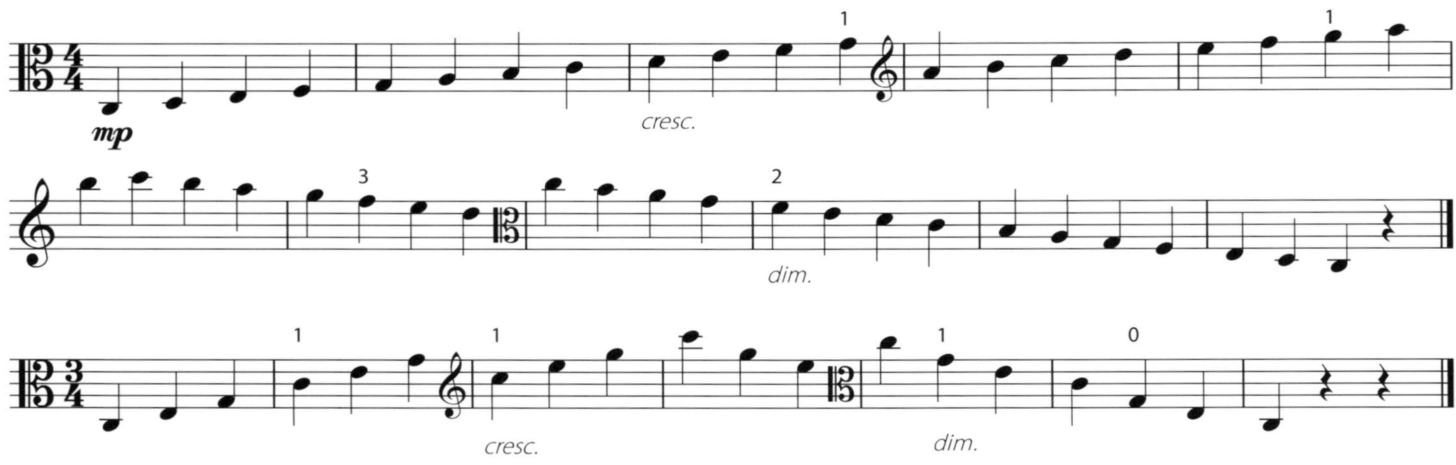

In this next study, notice that the first note of bars 1–5 is always the same C.

When changing clef be mindful of the first note and then focus on the intervals.

Study No. 1 Op. 45

Franz Wohlfahrt

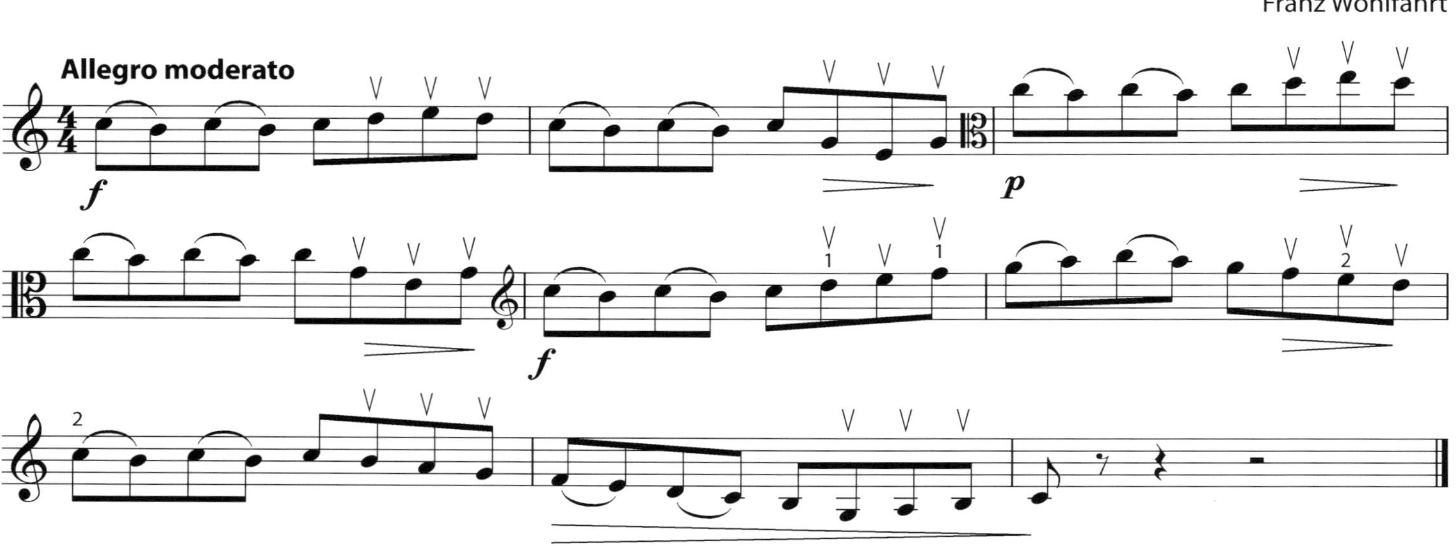

This study uses only the treble clef.

Arpeggio study

Otakar Ševčík

Here is a famous piece to practise clef changes and position work.

Theme from Caprice No. 24

Quasi presto

Niccolò Paganini

ACTIVITY BOX

Name the following notes *as quickly as you can*, then play them:

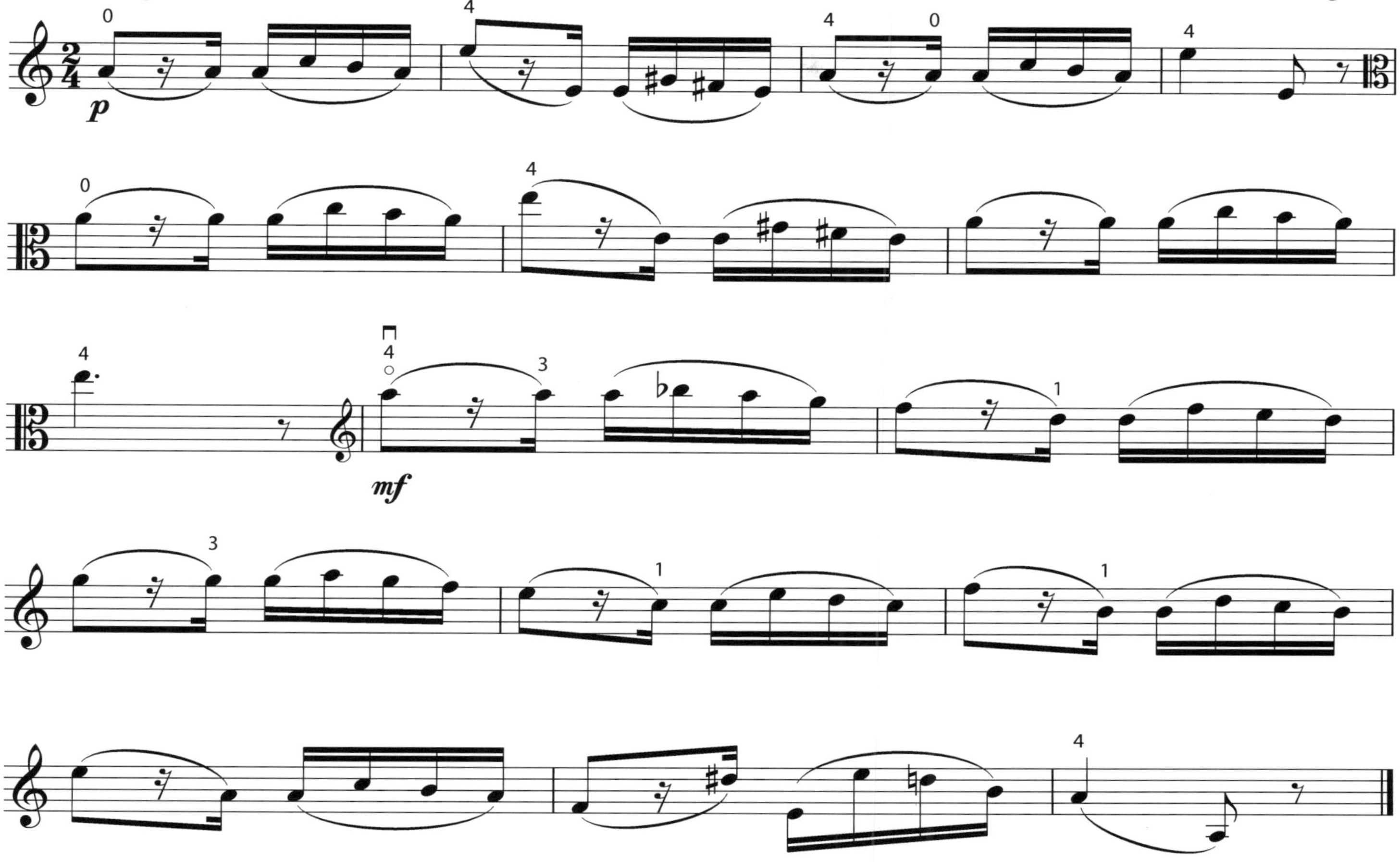

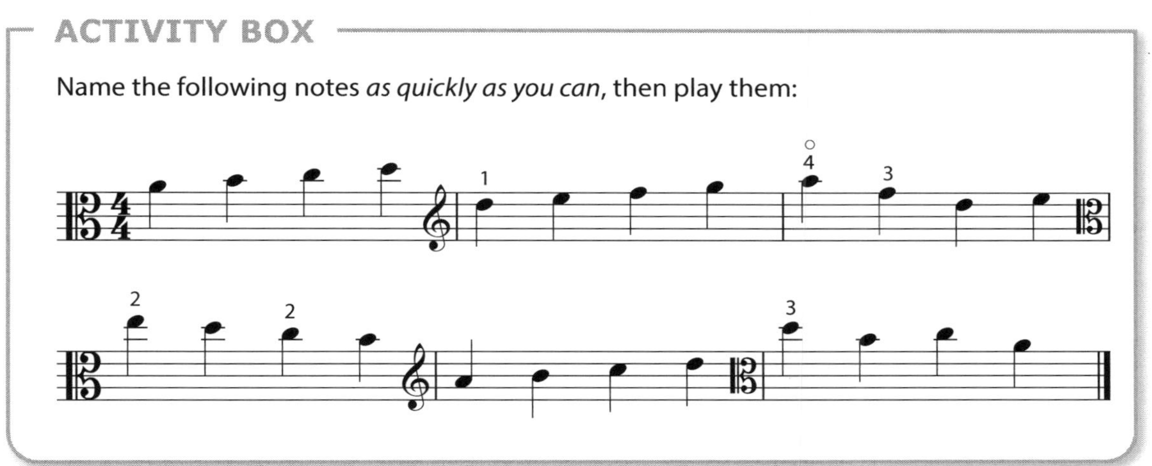

One of the joys of playing the viola is that we can play music from both the violin and cello repertoire.

Here are the opening bars from a famous Cello Prelude by Bach, which works beautifully on the viola. This is now core repertoire for the viola, so it is worth having your own copy – there are a number of excellent editions available.

Prelude from Cello Suite No. 1

Play this beautiful tune with your best sound and vibrato. Find a copy of the full movement to play later.

Air from Suite No. 3

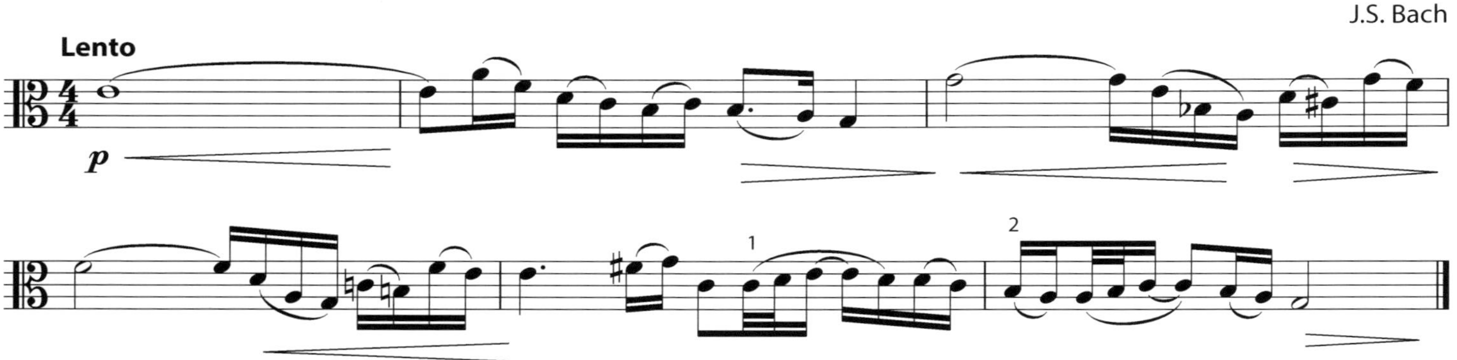

ACTIVITY BOX

Now that you are comfortable with shifting and position work, go back to earlier pieces from Stage 2 onwards and add your own shifts to limit the open strings and increase the resonance of the sound.

Playing chromatic notes, *pizzicato* and double stops

For *pizzicato* on the viola you'll need to press your left-hand fingers down a little more so that the string makes firm contact with the fingerboard. With the right hand, use the fleshy part of the 1st or 2nd finger and move the arm outwards towards the scroll.

Exercise 14 Practise this next series of exercises *arco* and then *pizzicato*.

Below are three options for fingering chromatic notes. If you have a larger viola, consider using the second or third suggestions. Choose the fingering that suits you best for the fourth line.

Enjoy playing this wonderful arrangement of Franck's Violin Sonata. Be prepared to stretch your fingers without straining. Feel free to add some slides to make it more stylish.

Theme from Sonata in A major, 2nd movement

César Franck

Mozart wrote two duos for violin and viola. Here is part of Mozart's String Duo No. 1.
Play it with your teacher or a friend and make sure you have a go playing each line.

String Duo No. 1 Op. 28

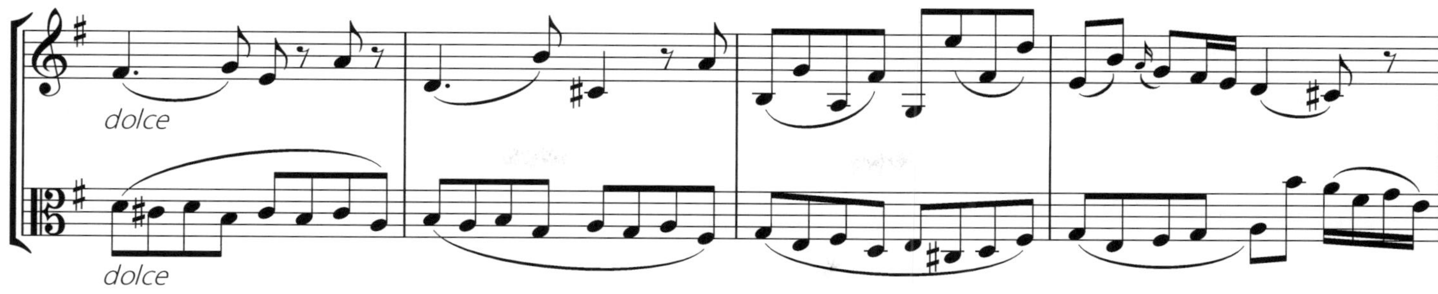

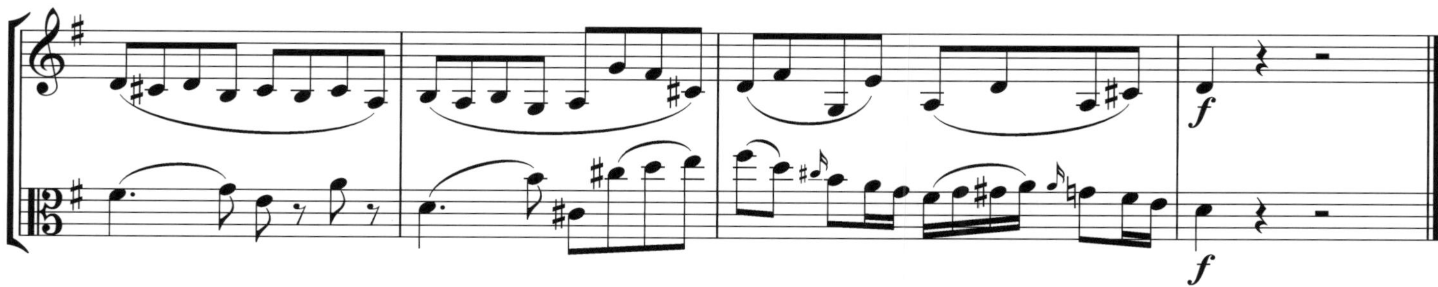

This exciting concerto by Malcolm Arnold uses lots of chromatic notes. There are a number of performances available online, so find one to listen to and enjoy.

Viola Concerto, 3rd movement

Malcolm Arnold

Enjoy this simple tune and match the ringing tone of the *arco* to the *pizzicato* as you move from one to the other.

Little brown jug

Joseph Winner

Exercise 15 Double stops are excellent for keeping the left handshape rounded and the bow parallel to the bridge. Be mindful to keep the left thumb relaxed.

Exercise 16 In these octaves check that your viola is resting comfortably on your collar bone and your left elbow is rotated for the lower strings to avoid any strain.

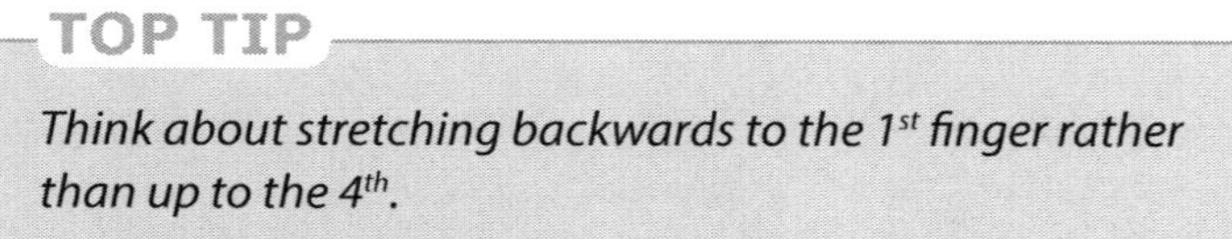

Here are two famous moments in Grieg's *Holberg Suite* where the viola section strongly features.

Holberg Suite

Edvard Grieg

Stage 10

What's next?

Much of the joy in playing the viola is being part of an ensemble or orchestra. Join a chamber group first if possible – you'll be able to hear yourself clearly. Once your understanding grows consider joining an orchestra where the music might be more complex. At first some occasional editing of the trickier passages is acceptable, but you'll soon develop the necessary skills and confidence.

Here are two important viola solos from famous works. Find the complete pieces to explore and listen to recordings.

Theme from *The Arpeggione*, 1st movement

Theme from *Sinfonia Concertante*, 2nd movement

Have a look at Berlioz's *Harold in Italy*, Rebecca Clarke's Viola Sonata, Schumann's *Märchenbilder* and *Viola Joke!* by Paul Harris.

The viola is of course one of the instruments in the string quartet – the repertoire is both vast and wonderful. Here are two short tasters. The first is from Haydn's 1st Quartet.

String Quartet No. 1, 1st movement

Joseph Haydn

The second is the theme from Dvořák's *American Quartet*:

Theme from *The American Quartet* Op. 96

Antonín Dvořák

Allegro ma non troppo

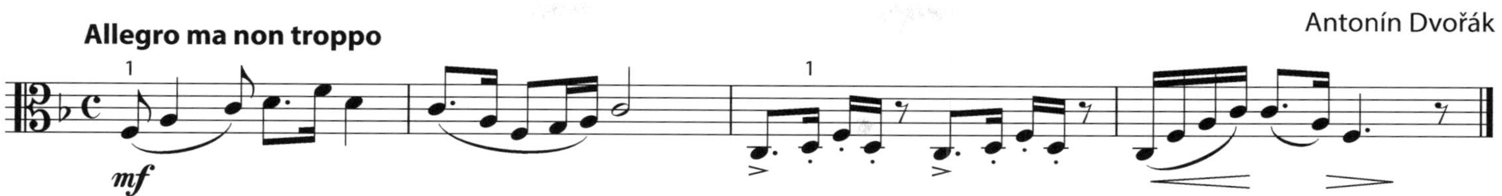

Here's an extract from Halvorsen's *Sarabande and variations* for violin and viola.

Sarabande and variations on a theme by Handel

Johan Halvorsen

Andante lento

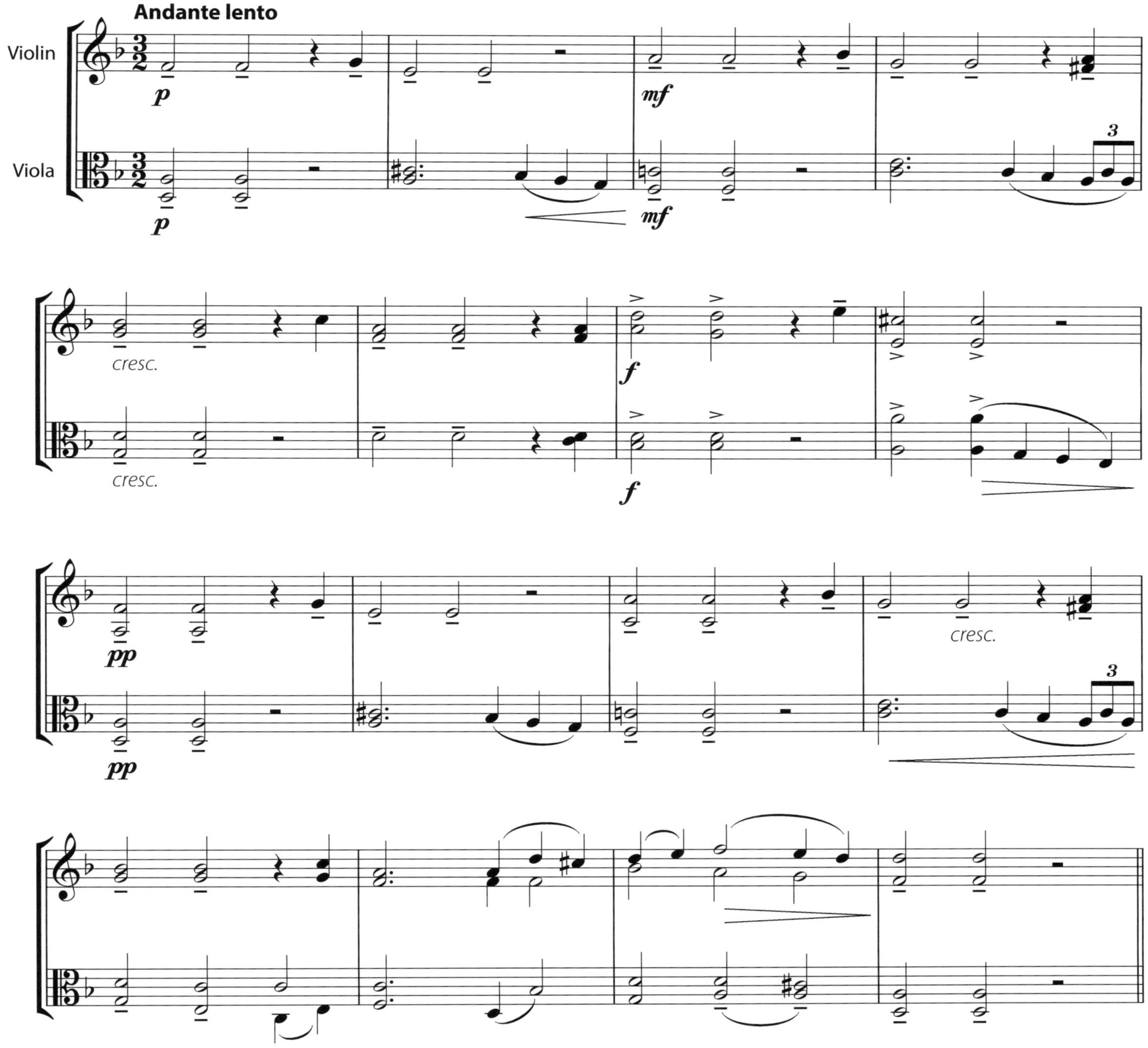

più mosso
p espress.
p espress.
pp
pp
mf
mf
cresc.
cresc.
f
f
p
p
cresc.
cresc.
p
p
36

Here is more from Mozart's String Duo No. 1. This is part of the 3rd movement. Have a go at playing both parts.

Rondo from Duo No. 1 Op. 28

W.A. Mozart

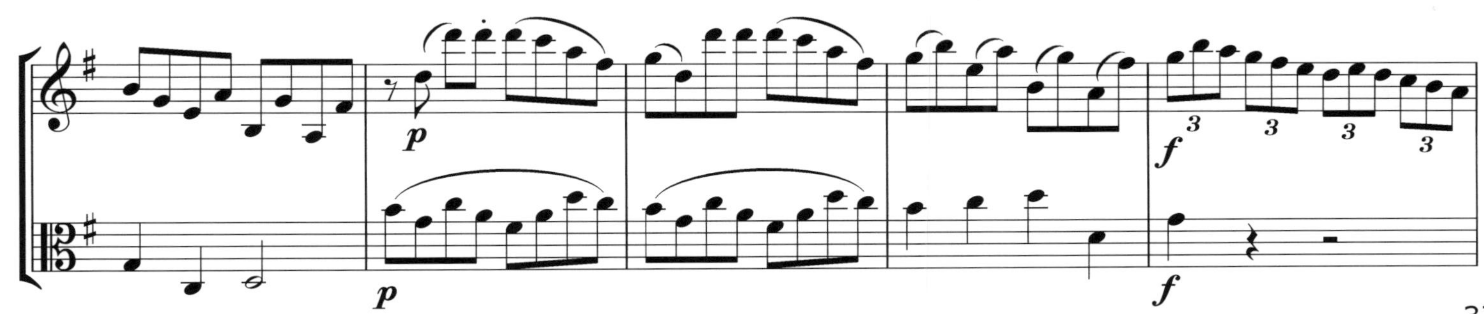

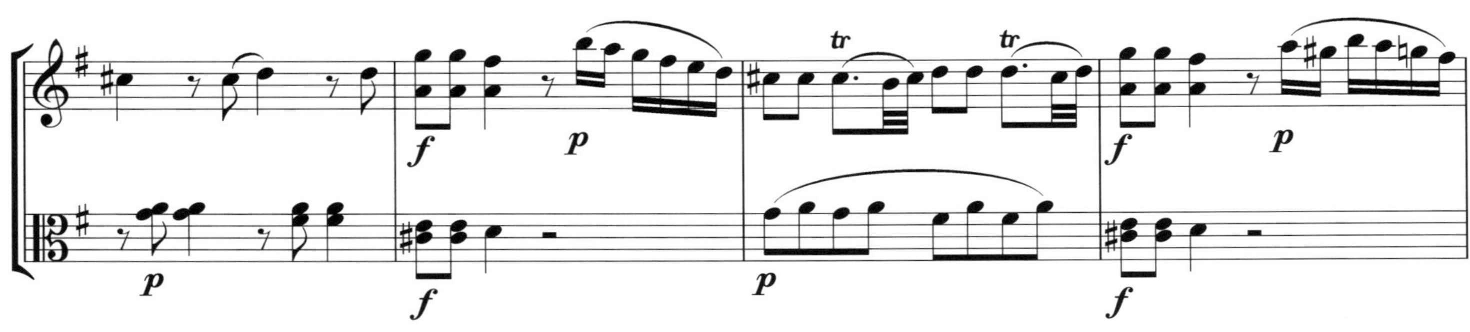

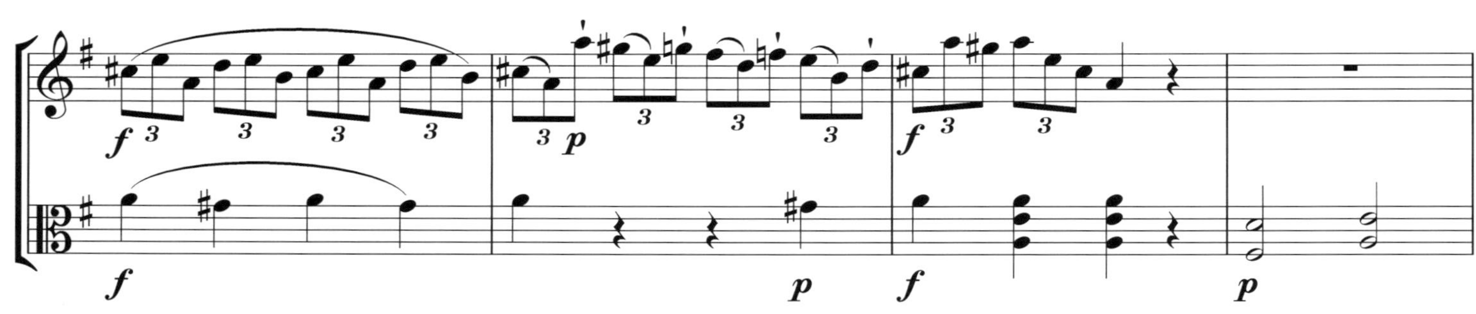

Rondo from Duet No. 1 for Two Violas

Here's a fun duet for two violas by the famous German composer Karl Stamitz who encouraged the frequent use of *crescendos* and *diminuendos* in performance. Add some to your performance of this piece.

Karl Stamitz

There are a number of great concertos for viola to listen to and eventually explore:

Malcolm Arnold	Concerto for Viola and Chamber Orchestra Op. 108
Max Bruch	Double Concerto in E minor for Clarinet, Viola and Orchestra Op. 88
Paul Hindemith	*Der Schwanendreher* ('The Swan Turner'), Concerto for Viola and Orchestra
J.N. Hummel	*Potpourri for Viola and Orchestra* Op. 94
Carl Philipp Stamitz	Viola Concerto in D major Op. 1
G.P. Telemann	Viola Concerto in G major TWV 51:G9
William Walton	Viola Concerto

Final thought ... don't stop playing the violin!